如是力若有眾生恭敬禮拜觀世音

不唐捐是故眾生皆應受持觀世音

等無盡意若有人受持六十二億恒

薩名字復盡形供養飲食衣服臥具

於汝意云何是善男子善女人功德多

不無盡意言甚多世尊佛言若復有人受持

觀世音菩薩名号乃至一時礼拜供養是二

人福正等無異於百千万億劫却不可窮盡無

佛在盒内

BUDDHA

佛
在
金
内

BUDDHA

BY MANUELA DUNN MASCETTI

CHRONICLE BOOKS

SAN FRANCISCO

Manufactured in China
Typeset in Bembo
ISBN 0-8118-1950-7

10 9 8 7 6

Distributed in Canada by
Raincoast Books
9050 Shaughnessy Street
Vancouver, B.C. V6P 6E5

Chronicle Books LLC
85 Second Street
San Francisco, CA 94105
www.chroniclebooks.com

Text by Manuela Dunn Mascetti
Design by Bullet Liongson

TABLE OF CONTENTS

INTRODUCTION

*S*ince Buddha's enlightenment twenty-five hundred years ago, Buddhist ethics and practices have adapted themselves remarkably well to the spiritual needs of modern humanity. Buddha is the embodiment of compassion with no other purpose than that of opening people up to their own potential for enlightenment.

This gift box you hold in your hands is a reminder of your own highest wisdom. Place it on the nightstand by your bed, on your home altar, on your desk at the office, on a shelf, or wherever it looks beautiful, and every time you look at it allow it to remind you of the unfolding of your consciousness toward Buddhahood. Ideally, the Buddha should sit peacefully in an open space so that his presence can create a field of energy, a space for you to change, an atmosphere of serenity and of trust that will help show you that the highest aspirations are indeed attainable. Buddha enfolds all things and all beings completely, and his presence in your life will introduce a new dimension of being and of relating.

Buddhists say that Buddha appears in your life only at certain moments, when one is in need of a reminder. Buddha can manifest as a friend, teacher, mother, father, or mentor. In this case, Buddha has manifested in this box and has come into your life for a specific purpose: to help you increase understanding and to improve emotions, perceptions, insights, and feelings.

May the power, wisdom, compassion, blessing, and enlightenment of Buddha be with you.

THE LEGEND OF AN AWAKENING BUDDHA

Yielding like the earth,
Joyous and clear like the lake,
Still as the stone at the door,
He is free from life and death.

His thoughts are still.
His words are still.
His work is stillness.
He sees his freedom and he is freed.

The master surrenders his beliefs.
He sees beyond the end and the beginning.

He cuts all ties.
He gives up all his desires.
He resists all temptation.
And he rises.

—THE DHAMMAPADA, VERSES 95–99

Siddhartha Gautama was born in 586 B.C.E. on the full moon in the month of May. His father, Suddhodana, was old and had been waiting many years for a child. He was the leader of the Shakya clan and lived in the foothills of the Himalayas. It was the custom at the time for the mother to travel to her parental home to give birth, so Gautama's mother, Mahamaya, was on her way to her parents' home. While resting in the Lumbini Gardens in Nepal, she gave birth to a boy and, without continuing her journey, she and the newborn child turned back and went home.

Within a day or two of the birth, a mystic called Kala Devala came down from the mountains to see the child. The seer was widely renowned for his wisdom and powers of clairvoyance. He was very old, but nevertheless he traveled a long distance to see the child. Legend tells that Gautama's mother had dreamed during her pregnancy of a white elephant, a mythical dream that foretells the birth of a *chakravartin,* a great emperor of the world. When Kala Devala looked at the newborn child, he first smiled, then wept, and finally bowed down to touch the child's feet. Suddhodana, the father, asked about this puzzling behavior and the old mystic replied, "I smiled when I saw him because I have been privileged to see a being who will know Buddhahood. Then I wept, because as I know my own future I know that I shall not live to meet him then. You should rejoice, Suddhodana, because the son that is born to you will become the greatest being in the whole world. This is no ordinary child."

Suddhodana wanted to test Kala Devala's reading, so he brought in eight astrologers. They looked at the child and then all except one raised their hands and pointed two fingers in the air. Suddhodana did not understand. When he asked them to explain their sign, they said that the child was very rare and that he had a great future. They were undecided about this future, however, because they could see two possibilities— therefore the two fingers. The destiny of the child was not fixed. But the eighth astrologer, Kondanna, saw only one destiny: "A time will come when this child will see four special signs. As a result of this he will renounce the world and go out and seek enlightenment. Eventually he will attain this and he will become a great Buddha." Kondanna himself was so impressed by the child that he left the palace of Suddhodana to renounce the world, and together with four friends decided to wait for the child to grow up and attain his enlightenment.

It was a custom at that time for a child's name to be determined by Brahman priests, so they were called in and chose the name Siddhartha, which means "the fulfillment of desire." Suddhodana felt this to be a very appropriate name for his son and successor. This child was indeed a powerful realization of the king's desire. He was so impressed by the possibility that this child would become a great emperor that at first he did not pay much attention to the second possibility. He could not imagine that his son would renounce such a kingdom as the predictions said he would. But it was not long before he became troubled by the prediction that Siddhartha would give up everything to become a Buddha. Again, he called the astrologers and asked for advice. They said that the future depended upon Suddhodana: in order to guarantee his son's future as a great emperor and to keep him from renouncing life, he must safeguard him from knowing that life consists of misery, suffering, pain, sickness, old age, and death. If Suddhodana could protect his child from realizing

that certain individuals forsake life in order to seek
enlightenment, then the child would become an emperor.
He was told that the ultimate destiny of Siddhartha was
in his hands. They suggested that the child should be
surrounded with as much luxury and comfort as possible
so as not to feel the miseries of life. They told the king
that he should gather the most beautiful women around
his son so that he would not feel lonely, and that
Suddhodana should make beautiful palaces for him in
different parts of the kingdom for each of the different
seasons so that his son would not feel bored. They went
into great detail as to how the life of this child should
be guided. He should never see anything sick, old, or
dying. He should never see a dying leaf or an aging
plant. No old man or old woman should be allowed
to enter into his palaces. And it was very important
that special arrangements be made for his travels, lest
a monk or ascetic of any sort cross his path.

Suddhodana was determined to follow all of
the astrologers' suggestions. He surrounded Siddhartha
with luxury and had several palaces built for him with
impeccably kept gardens filled with flowering plants—
any that were dying were immediately taken away. No

old or dying people were allowed near the prince. His life was filled with beauty. At age sixteen, Siddhartha married the exquisite princess Yashodara and went on to lead a life of utter pleasure. Every care was taken that Siddhartha would see nothing that could cause him to question that which was around him.

It was part of the young Siddhartha's duty to inaugurate the Youth Festival that took place every spring. In his twenty-ninth year, the prince went out for a carefully planned drive as he had done many times before, except this time, the gods determined to outwit the efforts of Suddhodana. Not wanting to miss the flowering of a great Buddha, they intervened in Siddhartha's fate and showed him the Four Sights.

Chonna, Siddhartha's loyal coachman, drove the prince through the city and out into the country to the festival. Chonna was well practiced at avoiding any of the miseries of life, but this time the gods ensured that Siddhartha saw what he had avoided before. First he saw a man bent over with age. Since he had never seen anyone old before, he asked Chonna to explain. "You have been prevented from seeing people growing old," replied Chonna. "But everybody gets old, it is the way of

life. This man was once a youth full of life and energy, but now that years have passed the strength of his life is wasted. Just as from childhood you have become a young man, from youth you will one day become old." Siddhartha thought to himself, "What is the point then of any pleasure when I know that I will soon wither and pine away?" This was the wisdom of the First Sight.

Next he saw a sick man on the side of the road. Puzzled, Siddhartha again asked Chonna to explain. "It is a law of nature that we are all prone to sickness. Poor, rich, ignorant, or wise, we are all creatures with bodies and so liable to disease. This man is sick and nothing can be done about it," replied Chonna. Sickness was the Second Sight.

Soon after, they saw four people carrying a corpse. Siddhartha asked Chonna what they were carrying and why they were so overwhelmed with grief. Chonna answered, "They are carrying a dead man. His body is stiff; his life gone. His family and the friends who loved him now grieve for him as they carry his corpse to the grave." Siddhartha asked if he, too, would one day die. Chonna explained, "He who begins life must end it. Your father is going to die, I am going to die, you are going to die. Death begins the day you are born." Death was the Third Sight.

Finally, while driving back to the palace, they met a monk, his head shaven, wearing a saffron robe and carrying a begging bowl. Siddhartha again asked Chonna to explain. "He has understood that beauty will turn to ugliness, youth into old age, life into death, and he is looking for the eternal, looking for that which does not die. Renouncing the ordinary world, he is a seeker of truth." This encounter was the Fourth Sight.

Siddhartha, upon returning to the palace, said to Chonna: "I have become sick. I have become old. I have died. I have tasted the sorrow of man. I want to find that which remains untouched by these realities. What does it matter if old age is still far ahead of me? Soon it will walk by my side. I don't want to be like that dead man. There is no more time to waste. I want to find out the cause of this suffering and find liberation from it."

When he returned home, Siddhartha was told of the birth of his son. He thought that his son, who he named Rahul, would prevent him from embarking on his search for truth. Rahul in Indian mythology is one of the two enemies of the moon. When there is an eclipse, it is because Rahul and Ketu have caught the moon and are trying to kill it. "Rahul," Siddhartha thought, "will try to destroy me."

Siddhartha awoke in the middle of the night. His resolve had crystallized and he decided to leave at once. He woke Chonna and told him to ready a horse. Before he left, he crept into his wife's chamber and became consumed with anguish at leaving behind those he loved. Resolutely, he left the palace and rode away in the night with Chonna at his side, determined to find an answer to the Four Sights.

Having put plenty of distance between himself and the palace, Siddhartha dismounted, cut off all his hair, undressed, and gave everything to Chonna, who was in tears and could not understand what Siddhartha was doing. The prince said to him, "Chonna, all living things must part. Let us do so now of our own accord; in due course death will tear us apart and we will have no say in the matter." So he left Chonna behind and traveled alone. His search had begun.

Since I ate so little my body reached a state of extreme emaciation. My limbs became like the

木曾海道六拾九次之内　板鼻

dry and knotted joints of bamboo. My buttocks
became like a buffalo's hoof, and my spine with
its protruding vertebrae looked like a string of
beads. My ribs were visible like the exposed
rafters of a dilapidated house. Just as in a deep
well the surface of the water gleams far below,
so my pupils, sunk deep in their sockets,
gleamed far below. (*from* THE VOICE OF BUDDHA)

Siddhartha spent years fasting and practicing the
most extreme ascetic disciplines, and still he had not
found a way of transcending the fate shown him by the
Four Sights. One day, after meditating on the banks of
the Niranjana, a nearby stream, he took a bath. Afterward
he found that he was so weak he could hardly pull
himself out of the shallow waters—fasting was killing
him and bringing him no closer to enlightenment. By
chance, a woman came by and brought a bowl of milk
as an offering in her worship of the holy tree under
which Siddhartha was sitting. Believing him to be the
god of the tree, the woman offered him the milk. And it
was thus that after years of discipline Siddhartha ate and
bathed again. That night he slept peacefully, abandoning

all longing for enlightenment and liberation. He now had
no desire, no longing, no future, no hope. Everything
was shattered. He slept a dreamless sleep, as though
without a mind. When he awoke in the morning, just
as the last star was setting, he suddenly became full of
awareness. From sleep he had awakened into full
consciousness. From the emptiness of the night before,
a great awareness had arisen in him, bringing him a sense
of immortality, eternity, serenity, silence, blissfulness,
and ecstasy he had not imagined. He called the state of
the night *anatta*—no self, emptiness, the void. He called
the state of the morning *nirvana*—blowing out the
candle.

And it was thus that a great Buddha awakened
on earth.

THE WAY OF THE MASTER

You are as the yellow leaf.
The messengers of death are at hand.
You are to travel far away. What will you take with you?

You are the lamp
To lighten the way.
Then hurry, hurry.

When your light shines
Without impurity or desire
You will come into the boundless country.
Your life is falling away.
Death is at hand.
Where will you rest on the way?
What have you taken with you?

You are the lamp
To lighten the way.
Then hurry, hurry.

When your light shines purely
You will not be born
And you will not die.

—THE DHAMMAPADA, VERSES 235–238

In his enlightenment, Buddha did not remain a solitary figure, far away from the world of humanity. On the contrary, he left the place where enlightenment had come to him and went in search of his first disciples. This was his initial lesson in compassion: to share his fullness with the world. To become a Buddha is to become completely open to a tremendous energy that we call grace, beauty, love. In Sanskrit, to be in the presence of Buddha is called *satsang,* literally meaning "to be in the presence of truth." The awakened one is like a deep well; those who are thirsty do not drink from their own well because they do not know how, so they search for a Buddha to teach them. The thirsty man sits in the presence of the awakened one and drinks from the source. Buddha offered his first disciples *satsang*— sitting with him in meditation so that the grace of one would flow into the other. He also offered *darshan,* which literally means "to have the experience of seeing through the eyes of the mystic." This is the moment when one has an experiential understanding of one's own truth in the presence of the mystic. *Satsang* and *darshan* are the mystical methods of the enlightened one. Just as the cloud, heavy with

rainwater, begins to shower, so Gautama Buddha began to share his experience.

He went in search of the four friends who had left him weeks before because he had eaten food, believing that he had abandoned his search for enlightenment and his life of asceticism. Still feeling resentful, they rebuffed and mocked him. But it was not long before they too were enveloped in the peace and calm in which Buddha was standing. As they sat with Buddha they understood what had happened to him; they knew he had become enlightened and that from him they could taste what they had been longing for. They bent down and touched his feet, opened their hearts to him, sat with him, and drank from his deep silence.

The first series of talks by Buddha to his disciples came to be known as *Sermon of the Turning of the Wheel of Dharma,* or *Dhammapada* in Pali, the ancient language of the Buddhist scriptures. *Dharma* is a Sanskrit word (*Dhamma* in Pali) that means the existential way of things, the ultimate law, the ultimate reality, the way things are. The Sanskrit root of the word is DHR, literally meaning "to support, to remain," so it gives a sense of a moral and spiritual law based upon ultimate truth. The word *pada,* both in Sanskrit and Pali, means "foot, step" and hence has the meaning of a path. *Dhammapada* is the path of Dharma, the right path of life, of light, and of love that leads us to enlightenment. Turning the wheel of Dharma is a way of saying that as Buddha began to speak he gave the wheel of evolving consciousness a new turn, and so began an age in which Buddha turned humanity toward himself and religion became a deeply personal experience ungoverned by any outside priest. He invited his disciples to enter a new experiment with him. In the intimacy of the first days he said, "This is what happened to me; I will teach you."

> *The perfume of flowers goes not against the wind,*
> *not even the perfume of sandalwood, of rosebay,*
> *or of jasmine; but the perfume of virtue travels*
> *against the wind and reaches into the ends of the*
> *world.* (THE DHAMMAPADA, VERSE 54)

The perfume of virtue can be inhaled when we practice the four great jewels of Buddhism — the Four Virtues: *Maitri, Karuna, Mudita,* and *Upeksha. Maitri* is friendliness, goodwill, benevolence, loving-kindness to all. *Karuna* is compassion, pity, and sorrow for the suffering of all.

Mudita is joy in the goodness of all. And, finally, *Upeksha* is forgiveness, compassion for the faults of all. Seeing and recognizing the Four Virtues is a vision of purity, known as *right views,* and the first step in Buddha's Eightfold Path to Enlightenment.

The second step is *right determination* — pure intentions upon starting the path to enlightenment make us fit to attain the goal.

The third step is *right words* — the *Dhammapada* tells us that "better than a thousand useless words is one word that gives us peace."

The fourth step is *right action* — this is good and pure work that is engaged in as an offering of love.

The fifth step is *right livelihood* — using the right means to support one's life, or not working for the production and use of things that are useless, harmful, or evil.

The sixth step is *right effort* — the proper balance between tension and relaxation, approaching everything with a balanced attitude.

The seventh step is *right remembrance* — remembering our true nature and that silence and stillness dwell at the center of our being.

And, finally, the eighth and last step is *samadhi*—communion, enlightenment, the drop merging with the ocean, the end of suffering that comes when "the traveler has reached the end of the journey" (THE DHAMMAPADA, VERSE 90).

The Eightfold Way and the Four Virtues are pinned upon the four universal truths that Buddha saw when he attained *samadhi:* life without awareness is misery; the cause of misery is desire; to let go of desire one needs to be aware; to be aware is the way. The Way of Buddha is also called the "middle path"—not swerving one way or another, but remaining level and moving through life with deepening awareness.

The way is Eightfold
There are Four Truths
All virtue lies in detachment.

The Master has an open eye.
This is the only way,
The only way to the opening of the eye.
Follow it.
Outwit desire.
Follow it to the end of sorrow.

—THE DHAMMAPADA, VERSES 273–278

Buddha told his disciples one simple thing: "Watch the tracks of desire. Be still and know. Then you will see how things are." He spent the first rainy season at Deer Park, a beautiful wooded spot in the north of India. For the next forty-two years, he walked from village to village, speaking to everyone who would listen to him, gathering a huge number of disciples, and building his *sangha*, his new community. He initiated thousands of people as *bhikkhus*, disciples who left their businesses and families to live with Buddha as their master.

THE PSYCHOLOGY OF THE BUDDHAS

The essence of Buddhist culture is defined by the experience of real Buddhas living among millions of disciples. From the beginning, Buddhists have taken for granted the constant presence of many enlightened individuals living among them. The *satori* of Gautama Buddha was transmitted first to his disciples, who also became enlightened, and then from one lineage to the next in a long tradition that stretches for centuries. Buddhism is a reorientation of the individual and community life to account for the existence of enlightened beings, the possibility of becoming one, and the actuality of a methodical process for doing so.

Tibetan Buddhism in particular has preserved the huge treasury of original Indian Buddhist experience.

For Tibetans, Buddhas are not gods or objects of belief.
They are real manifestations, real souls who incarnate
in human form, who have transcended death and are
thus utterly available to their people. His Holiness the
Fourteenth Dalai Lama of Tibet is the reincarnation
of the Buddha of Compassion, and one of his titles is
Ocean of Wisdom. The Dalai Lama is simultaneously
the supreme religious figurehead for Tibetans and the
highest seat of political power. In Tibetan culture, the
wisdom and compassion of the reincarnated Buddha
also represents the maximum political authority, for no
other being could lead the people toward the right path.
In the specific context of Tibet, the moral and spiritual
authority of the Dalai Lama has waged a nonviolent
fight to preserve Tibetan culture and identity in the
face of Chinese occupation.

The psychological paradigm that Gautama
Buddha presented for humanity extends in the opposite
direction from the paradigm offered by Western
psychology. Through meditation, and by following the
Four Noble Truths, the Four Virtues, and the Eightfold
Path, a disciple becomes intimately acquainted with the
psychology of enlightenment and the transcendence of

mind. Western psychology studies the layers beneath the
conscious mind, whereas in Buddhism one has a direct
experience of the layers *above* the conscious mind. The
very existence of Buddhas among ordinary people gives
us a taste of the full flowering of an individual.

The enlightenment of Buddha was not primarily
a religious discovery or a mystical encounter with God.
It was an individual's direct, exact, and final discovery
of the structure of reality and of the ultimate nature of
being. A Buddha's mind is what we might think of God's
mind as being like. However, it rests within a human
body, and frames the possibility of Buddhahood for
each individual. "Buddha" is not a title, but simply a
statement of fact: the awakened one, the enlightened
one, the evolved.

The last word that Gautama Buddha uttered
before he died was *sammasati:* remember that you are
a Buddha. In everything you do, in everything you
feel, in everything you think, in every movement of
consciousness—remember that you are a Buddha.

The psychology of Buddhism thus proposes
a radical shift of paradigm: every life has the purpose
of achieving supreme happiness through total awareness

of itself and of the universe. Every being has been working from time immemorial to perfect his or her nature over lifetimes. This fulfillment, this perfection, occurs by understanding, awareness, wisdom, watchfulness, and sensitivity. And the infinite number of beings who have already achieved perfect Buddhahood share that happiness and light with all other beings, showering us every second with infinite grace, beauty, love, and compassion. They become the guardians and friends who watch over us as we walk on the path. When Buddha addressed his disciples at the beginning of each sermon, he would call them, "My beloveds, my friends, my fellow travelers," and this is what Buddhas are to each one of us.

Buddhist education is therefore not a belief-based system, but rather an awakening in each individual, without indoctrination or conditioning. Education is based upon the contemplation and practice of enlightened tools: the sutras as the enlightened words of Gautama Buddha; prayers, blessings, and mantras as the showering of the wisdom of the Buddhas upon us and as a means of evoking their perfection within us.

THE SUTRAS

The word *sutra* in Sanskrit (and *sutta* in Pali) refers to the solemn utterances of the Buddha. Originally the word meant a string or thread; important words or brief phrases strung together were thus called sutras by analogy with the string or thread on which a garland of flowers is made — a collection of words with the fragrance of beauty.

The oldest compilations of the Buddha's sermons — the Five Nikayas of the Pali canon and the Four Agamas of the Chinese canon — are collectively called the *Sutra-pitaka*, or Sutra Basket. The monastic rules observed by Buddha's disciples and expounded by him are called the *Vinaya-pitaka*, or Ordinance

Basket. After his death, the leading disciples began to study and organize the Buddha's teachings theologically and philosophically, and composed commentaries called *Abhidharma-pitaka,* or Treatise Basket. Only the scriptures in the Sutra Basket are usually called sutras.

Mountain Falling Flowers

We accept the graceful falling
Of mountain cherry blossoms,
But it is much harder for us
To fall away from our own
Attachment to the world.

—BUDDHIST NUN RENGETSU

木曾街道

鵜沼驛従

犬山遠望

廣重画

Here, O Sariputra, form is emptiness

and emptiness is form;

emptiness does not differ from form,

form does not differ from emptiness;

whatever is form, that is emptiness,

whatever is emptiness, that is form;

the same is true of feelings, perceptions, impulses,

and consciousness.

Here, O Sariputra,

all dharmas are marked with emptiness;

they are not produced or stopped,

not defiled or immaculate,

not deficient or complete.

—THE HEART SUTRA

Therefore, O Sariputra,

in emptiness there is no form,

nor feeling, nor perception,

nor impulse, nor consciousness;

no eye, ear, nose, tongue, body, mind;

no forms, sounds, smells, tastes, touchables,

or objects of mind;

no sight-organ element, and so forth,

until we come to.

No mind-consciousness element;

there is no ignorance, no extinction of ignorance,

and so forth, until we come to.

There is no decay and death,

no extinction of decay and death.

There is no suffering, no origination,

no stopping, no path.

There is no cognition, no attainment,

and no non-attainment.

—THE HEART SUTRA

Therefore, O Sariputra,

it is because of his non-attainment that a bodhisattva,

through having relied on the perfection of wisdom,

dwells without thought-coverings.

In the absence of thought-coverings

he has not been made to tremble,

he has overcome what can upset,

and in the end he attains nirvana.

All those who appear as Buddhas

in the three periods of time

are fully awake to the utmost, right, and perfect enlightenment

because they have relied on the perfection of wisdom.

—THE HEART SUTRA

What we are today, comes from our thoughts of yesterday,

and our present thoughts build our life of tomorrow:

our life is the creation of our mind.

If a man acts or speaks with an impure mind,

suffering follows him as the wheel of the cart follows

the beast that draws the cart.

What we are today comes from our thoughts of yesterday,

and our present thoughts build our life of tomorrow:

our life is the creation of our mind.

If a man speaks or acts with a pure mind,

joy follows him as his own shadow.

—THE DHAMMAPADA, VERSES 1–2

When a man knows the solitude of silence,

and feels the joy of quietness, he is then free from fear and sin

and he feels the joy of the dharma.

—THE DHAMMAPADA, VERSE 205

If you find a man who is constant, awake to the inner light,

learned, long-suffering, endowed with devotion, a noble

man—follow this good and great man even as

the moon follows the path of the stars.

—THE DHAMMAPADA, VERSE 208

PRAYERS, BLESSINGS, AND MANTRAS

One of the astonishing things about Buddhist culture in all its different traditions is the vastness of its literature. Radiating from the words of Buddha himself are hundreds of collections by eminent scholars, saints, sages, reincarnated Buddhas, masters, disciples, and ordinary people who follow the path in their everyday lives. Selecting texts from this wealthy treasury is by no means an easy task, and included here are but a very few examples of texts used for worship — a key practice of using words and rituals to awaken the Buddha within.

Prayers, blessings, and mantras are essentially offerings and invitations; in practicing them we gain appreciation of the evolutionary opportunity in human life. They help us renounce mundane preoccupations and instead develop the loving mind of the spirit of enlightenment. In the section at the back of the book titled "Further Reading List" you can find many more titles that illustrate how full our universe is of the Buddha presence.

PRAYERS

May all beings be happy and have the causes of happiness;

May all beings be free from suffering and the causes of suffering;

May all beings never be separated

from the great joy beyond suffering;

May they always remain in the great equanimity

beyond attachment or aversion.

—DAILY PRAYER RECITED BY MAHAYANA BUDDHISTS

Free from mental creation, it is Mahamudra.

Free from extremes, it is the Great Middle Way.

Being all-inclusive, it is also called the Great Perfection.

May we gain certainty that by knowing one,

all meanings are realized.

—TIBETAN PRAYER

By this virtue, may I quickly attain the state of vajradhara,

The whole essence of all Buddhas!

And may all beings attain it too!

May I practice all deeds for the sake of enlightenment,

the deeds taught by both the perfect Buddhas and by

Bodhichittavarja!

—Tibetan communal prayer

O all-time Buddhas with your children and disciples,

Your glory and ocean of boundless virtues,

You think of poor beings as each and only child;

Please attend to my truthful lamentation!

May you magnify the ten virtuous practices

Of the wise, adept upholders of the Buddha teaching,

And spread the glory of its benefit and bliss

the whole world over

As it abolishes the miseries of existence and extinction!

May you rescue wretched beings, ceaselessly tormented

By the fierce push of unbearably vicious evolutionary acts,

Prevent the horrors of their dread diseases, wars, and famines,

And restore their spirits in your ocean of bliss and happiness!

Please look upon the religious people of the Land of Snows,

Ruthlessly conquered with harsh tactics by malevolent invaders,

May your compassion exert itself with miraculous speed

To stop the torrent of their blood and tears!

Ah! Those cruel people defeat themselves as well as others,

Driven to insane behavior by the devil of addictive passions;

Have mercy and restore their decent insight of right and wrong,

Use love and kindness to reunite them in the

glory of human friendship!

Bring us our deep desire so long held in our secret hearts

The natural glory of the perfect freedom of the whole of Tibet,

And grant us the good fortune to enjoy once more

The millennial feast of the union of secular and sacred!

—PRAYER OF THE WORD OF TRUTH, BY HIS HOLINESS
THE FOURTEENTH DALAI LAMA

The nature of every sentient being is Buddha,

But because they don't recognize it,

They circle in the sufferings of samsara,

May I develop pure compassion, Limitless One,

towards all sentient beings.

—KARMAPA PRAYER, FROM THE LINEAGE OF BODHISATTVAS
BELIEVED TO BE REINCARNATIONS OF AVALOKITESHVARA

BLESSINGS

Then bless me to embark on the boat

to cross the ocean of the Tantras,

Through the kindness of the captain Vajra-master,

Holding vows and pledges, root of all powers,

More dearly than life itself!

Bless me to perceive all things as the deity body,

Cleansing the taints of ordinary perception and conception

Through the yoga of the first stage of Unexcelled Tantra,

Changing birth, death, and between

into the three Buddha bodies.

—TIBETAN BLESSING

Bless me to realize here in this life
The path of clear light body communion,
Coming from you, Savior, when you put your toe
In my eight-petaled heart-center!

If the path is not complete and death arrives,
Bless me to go to a pure Buddhaverse
By the instruction of implementing the five forces
Of mentor-soul-ejection, the forceful art of Buddhahood!

In short, life after life forever,
You, Savior, please care for me never apart,
Bless me to become your foremost child,
Upholding all the secrets of body, speech, and mind!

You, Savior, at your perfect Buddhahood,

May I be foremost in your retinue—

Grant me good luck for easy spontaneous achievement

Of all my goals, temporary and ultimate!

Thus having prayed, may you, Supreme Mentor

Joyously come to my crown to bless me,

Sit surely, your toenails glistening,

In the pistil of my heart-center lotus!

—BLESSING FROM THE TIBETAN QUINTESSENCE SEGMENT

MANTRAS

Then the transcendent Lord Padmottama, the Saint,
the perfectly enlightened Buddha, spoke to the Bodhisattva
Avalokiteshvara: "Give me, gentle son, the queen, the great
science of the six-syllable mantra with which I may liberate from
suffering hundreds of thousands of millions of billions of various
beings, so that I may cause them to reach unexcelled perfect
enlightenment as swiftly as possible."

Then the Bodhisattva Avalokiteshvara, the great spiritual
hero, gave the great science, the six-syllable mantra, to the
perfectly enlightened Buddha, the Transcendent Lord, the Saint
Padmottama:

OM MA NI PAD ME HUM

—INSTRUCTION IN THE GREAT SCIENCE OF THE SIX-SYLLABLE MANTRA

The very body of all Buddhas

Being fulfilled by my five aggregates,

By the reality of the Buddha Body,

May I also become just such!

OM SARVA TATHAGATA KAYA VAJRA SVABHAVA

ATMAKO HAM

—MANTRA FOR BLESSING THE BODY AS BUDDHA-BODY

The very speech of the Vajra Dharma,

Perfection of the definitive word,

May my word be also just such,

may I be like you, the Dharma Holder!

OM SARVA TATHAGATA VAGVAJRA SVABHAVA

ATMAKO HAM

—MANTRA FOR BLESSING THE SPEECH AS BUDDHA-SPEECH

The very Mind of Total Goodness,

With the genius of the Mystic Lord,

may I also become just such,

An equal of the Vajra Holder!

OM SARVA TATHAGATA KAYAVAKCHITTA

VAJRASVABHAVATMAKOHAM

—MANTRA FOR BLESSING THE MIND AS BUDDHA-MIND

BIBLIOGRAPHICAL REFERENCES

Bays, Gwendolyn. *The Voice of Buddha*. Boulder, CO:
   Dharma Publishing, 1983.

Conze, Edward, trans. *Buddhist Wisdom Books*. London:
   Unwin Hyman, 1988.

Foster, Nelson, and Jack Shoemaker. *The Roaring Stream*.
   Hopewell, NJ: The Ecco Press, 1996.

Mascaró, Juan, trans. *The Dhammapada*. London: Penguin
   Books, 1973.

Mizuno, Kogen. *Buddhist Sutras*. Tokyo: Kosei
   Publishing, 1982.

Tai Situpa. *Awakening the Sleeping Buddha*. Boston and
   London: Shambhala, 1996.

Thurman, Robert A.F. *Essential Tibetan Buddhism*.
   New York and San Francisco: HarperCollins, 1995.

FURTHER READING LIST

Peace Is Every Step by Thitch Nhat Hanh

Transformation and Healing by Thitch Nhat Hanh

The Miracle of Mindfulness by Thitch Nhat Hanh

A Still Forest Pool by Jack Kornfield and Paul Breiter

Living Buddhist Masters by Jack Kornfield

Zen Mind, Beginner's Mind by Shunryu Suzuki Roshi

The Sacred Path of the Warrior by Chogyam Trungpa

Cutting Through Spiritual Materialism by Chogyam Trungpa

The Path of Purification by Buddhagosa

The Zen Teachings of Rinzai translated by Irmgard Schloegl

The Buddhist Directory by Julie Foalkes

The Path of Compassion by Fred P. Eppsteiner

ACKNOWLEDGMENTS

Grateful acknowledgment is made for permission to reprint quotes from *The Dhammapada*, copyright © 1973 by Juan Mascaró, trans., reproduced by kind permission from Penguin Books, London. Quoted passages from the *Heart Sutra* are derived from *Buddhist Wisdom Books*, copyright © 1988 by Edward Conze, trans., and reprinted here by kind permission from Unwin Hyman, London. Mahayana Buddhist prayers on pages 64 and 66 are from *Awakening the Sleeping Buddha*, copyright © 1996 by the Twelfth Tai Situpa and reprinted here by kind permission from Shambhala Publications, London and Boston. Tibetan prayers and blessings appearing from page 68 through to page 82 are from *Essential Tibetan Buddhism*, copyright © 1995 by Robert A. F. Thurman, and are reproduced here by kind permission from HarperCollins, New York and San Francisco.

ART ACKNOWLEDGMENTS

BOX IMAGE: *Heike Nokyo,* Heike Family Votive Lotus Sutra, 1164;
© Itsukushima-jinja, Hiroshima

BOOK COVER: *Heike Nokyo,* Heike Family Votive Lotus Sutra, 1164;
© Itsukushima-jinja, Hiroshima

END PAPERS: *Heike Nokyo,* Heike Family Votive Lotus Sutra, 1164;
© Itsukushima-jinja, Hiroshima (another version)

PAGE 2: © The British Museum, London

PAGE 4-5: *Pine Trees in the Four Seasons* by Kano Tan 'Yu;
© Daitokuji, Kyoto

PAGE 6: *Seated Amida,* hanging scroll, Kamakura period, first half of the
14th century, Japan; © Asian Art Museum, San Francisco

PAGE 10: © The British Museum, London

PAGE 15: © The British Museum, London

PAGE 18: *Five Buddhists Avators of the Kasuga Gods* by Kasuga Honjibutsu
Mandala, Muromachi period, 15th century, Japan; © Asian Art
Museum, San Francisco

PAGE 22-23: © The British Museum, London

PAGE 26: *Sho-Kanno* (Avalokitesvara), late Heian period, 12th century,
Japan; © Asian Art Museum, San Francisco

PAGE 29: *Fifty-two Stages of the Tokkaido* by Utagawa Hiroshige;
© Tokyo National Museum, Tokyo

PAGE 32-33: *Flowers and Trees of the Four Seasons* by Watanabe Shiko;
© Hatakeyama Collection, Tokyo

PAGE 37: © The British Museum, London

PAGE 38: *White Tara,* 15th-16th century, Nepal; © Asian Art Museum,
San Francisco

PAGE 41: © The British Museum, London

PAGE 44: *White Phoenix in an Old Pine Tree* by Ito Jakuchu; © Museum of the Imperial Collections, His Majesty the Emperor of Japan, Kyoto

PAGE 47: © The British Museum

PAGE 48-49: © The British Museum, London

PAGE 51: © The British Museum, London

PAGE 52: © The British Museum, London

PAGE 55: © The British Museum, London

PAGE 57: © The British Museum, London

PAGE 59: *A True View of Mount Asama* by Aodo Denzen; © Tokyo National Museum, Tokyo

PAGE 60: © The British Museum, London

PAGE 63: *Water-wheel, Bridge, and Willow Tree in the Moonlight*; © Kyoto National Museum, Kyoto

PAGE 65: *Pine Trees in the Four Seasons* by Kano Tan 'Yu; © Daitokuji, Kyoto

PAGE 67: © The British Museum, London

PAGE 69: © The British Museum, London

PAGE 72: © The British Museum, London

PAGE 74: © The British Museum, London

PAGE 79: *Landscape* by Tani Buncho; © Tokyo National Museum, Tokyo

PAGE 81: © The British Museum, London

PAGE 83: © The British Museum, London

PAGE 84: © The British Museum, London

遶福德之利

無盡意菩薩白佛言世尊觀世音菩薩云何

遊此娑婆世界云何而為眾生說法方便之

方其事云何佛告無盡意菩薩善男子若有

國土眾生應以佛身得度者觀世音菩薩即

現佛身而為說法應以辟支佛身得度者即

現辟支佛身而為說法應以聲聞身得度者

即現聲聞身而為說法應以梵王身得度者